redirection

redirection
the prime sonnets and other poems

Brian T. W. Way

First Edition

Hidden Brook Press
www.HiddenBrookPress.com
writers@HiddenBrookPress.com

Copyright © 2015 Hidden Brook Press
Copyright © 2015 Brian T.W. Way

All rights for poems revert to the author. All rights for book, layout and design remain with Hidden Brook Press. No part of this book may be reproduced except by a reviewer who may quote brief passages in a review. The use of any part of this publication reproduced, transmitted in any form or by any means, electronic, mechanical, photocopied, recorded or otherwise stored in a retrieval system without prior written consent of the publisher is an infringement of the copyright law.

redirection: the prime sonnets and other poems
by Brian T. W. Way

Cover Design – Richard M. Grove
Layout and Design – Richard M. Grove

Typeset in Times New Roman
Printed and bound in USA

Library and Archives Canada Cataloguing in Publication

Way, Brian Thomas Wesley, 1951-, author
         Redirection : the prime sonnets and other poems / Brian T.W. Way.

ISBN 978-1-927725-20-7 (paperback)

         I. Title.

PS8645.A915R44 2015   C811'.6   C2015-904185-6

for Bob / for Bill

table of contents

– redirection – *p. 1*
– ode of sorts to purdy – *p. 2*
– pillars along the road – *p. 4*
– the fragile promise of november – *p. 7*
– the poppy – *p. 8*
– day fine but sky cloudy – *p. 9*
– to see the queen – *p. 19*
– alls right with the world – *p. 21*
– cassandra ex vicis – *p. 22*
– beautiful sacrifice – *p. 24*
– massacre at the metro – *p. 29*
– verge – *p. 31*
– the passage of seasons – *p. 33*
– heaven – *p. 35*
– barn fire – *p. 36*
– eulogy for an exotic pet owner – *p. 38*
– prehistoric literary note – *p. 39*
– the storms of my parents – *p. 40*
– asshole poem – *p. 43*
– descent of species – *p. 45*
– westview chapel on wonderland road – *p. 46*
– thunderbird bound in winter – *p. 48*
– teenager – *p. 50*
– guillotine troth – *p. 51*
– quarter days – *p. 52*
– middle ages – *p. 54*
– the hydro man – *p. 55*
– universal concrete poem – *p. 57*
– a prayer for my students – *p. 58*
– pieces of a butterfly – *p. 64*

the prime sonnets

– prologue – *p. 73*
– the grand old cat – *p. 74*
– one stone – *p. 76*
– lights in the north – *p. 78*
– o my annie – *p. 79*
– printers devil – *p. 80*
– the ram of cumberland – *p. 82*
– sunny ways – *p. 84*
– equality of sacrifice – *p. 85*
– old virtues – *p. 86*
– bonfire in the deluge – *p. 87*
– willy of the valley – *p. 88*
– loncle – *p. 89*
– the chief – *p. 90*
– mirrors – *p. 91*
– the rose – *p. 92*
– ahead of time – *p. 93*
– prepared – *p. 94*
– open for business – *p. 95*
– freak – *p. 96*
– smile of a tiger – *p. 97*
– family business – *p. 98*
– our dictatorship benign – *p. 100*
– epilogue – *p. 102*

Afterwords: the Sonnets – *p. 104*
The Prime Ministers of Canada – *p. 107*
Author Bio – *p. 108*

redirection

is the transforming   of i   into eye
a slow turning
toward seeing in the forensics of autumn   every absence
and finding in the metaphor that remains   a galaxy
autumn   the honestest season
    where the pure tree stands naked
a sacred second between past and future   living or other
and any moment   any moment
the dead snow can bury the land
like an eyelash bowing to a fleck of dust

even more than this   perceiving the pendular
the precise willability to move back and forth
    in space time form mood
to return to seed & emerge   return & emerge
    again & again
the still motion   the ineffable trick
    soul becoming root   tree   zygote
        autumn held in every pulse
a price   a human price surely
but alive
    in the only way to be scavenged in this mortal season
engraving on a profane canvas
    the invisible image of the visible thing

ode of sorts to purdy
(after first hearing al purdy read)

'keep your ass out of my beer'
he leaned across the podium
running freight car fingers through straight grey hair
attacking the audience as if they were all new romans
then he hesitated in his loping stance
retreating in memory to rummage out his solemn lines
'go ahead strike go ahead'

god damn it purdy move over
im from massassaga
thats only a couple miles from ameliasburg
    and wild grapes grow in plenty there too
and more important, i was born there
not in that damn dilapidated queens hotel
mired in the ghettoes of trenton
    where you gained breath
and my ancestor didnt just inherit roblins mill   he built it
agreed my village doesnt have some sort of freudian store
    with old women complaining about dirty poetry books
    the ones you tried to sell there a few years back
theres no lake either
but theres a marsh that the sun tries to glimmer across
    and where tall blue herons stand
so ive got my walden too
and experience with trains and hauling mattresses will come
but youve got books and canada council grants
and some pretty good poetry
more every time i turn around
    so i guess for now you bastard

      ill listen to you talk about
      the gold hairs on your wifes belly
      and your mice and your huskies and your pontiac
      your burning buildings your rhododendrons
      and the country of your defeat
but watch out   one of these days soon
im going to grow long straight grey hair
and drink beer all the time and
wear wrinkled white shirts with the sleeves rolled up
and believe me
      i can smoke those cheap white owls too

P.S.: Spring, 2000

silent now
your voice still resounds across the land it found
as for me, well cigars have gone quite out of public fashion
and long since ive been resigned never to catch up to you
but somehow in that defeat i find myself quite satisfied

pillars along the road

theyre building pillars along the road
obelisks of stone and brick and concrete
flanking the long rich driveways
    with a kind of magnanimous certitude
short or tall   thin or rotund
some little more than fat fence posts
but here and there extravagance roars up—
a set of serious lions obediently guards one drive
although as i travel by
they always seem a bit perplexed in tooth and claw
perhaps the errant vagueness of their assigned post
    confusing them
astride another drive, some unnameable creatures
a species of gargoyle or griffin or some beast
    from a fable yet to be written
they are contorted as if undergoing electric shock
    for what must be their ontological schizophrenia
or in discomfort from a stony bowel movement
    half-completed when their mould was cracked
there are no pillars in the shape of the creatures
that most inhabit this busy busy road
no squirrels or chipmunks or raccoons or kids on bicycles
    or old men driving young cars

some pillars have brass plaques with numbers or names
and some have lights to keep the day from dying
some are topped with flat bauhaus cubes
    or victorian coach lanterns
echoing some past that never was
    at least not here

but there are no gates   there are no fences
these great pillars crafted with such design and intent
     simply straddle open driveways
and would hold out only the most challenged
     of midnight burglars
defend against only the most drunken
   of wayward revolutionaries charging toward glory
   hasta la victoria siempre along county road number three
only to run smack into a random stone post in the mêlée
and what martyrdom for a stupid rebel
     with a headache and a hangover

and so the pillars stand alone
bistro cairns that keep things neither out nor in
exclamation marks to remind god
     of the wonder of his creation perhaps
like the holy pillars of old   the true boaz   the sure jachin
or just simple billboards to those passing by
here i begin   here i end
here i am beyond these unnatural piles of stone
i built this monument, or at least directed it so
i have the power to indulge in unnecessary things
to sculpt the mighty symmetry that resides in me
and announce this concupiscence so all can see
or perhaps they are cautionary signposts for those days
when the scent of mortality sweeps across the bay
and the cinder-man with certain stride seems close
touchstones that reveal something of our need
     to mark this fragile human journey

and remind us that everyone seeks redemption
    in one form or another
everyone needs redemption in one way or another

and so theyre building pillars along the road
obelisks of stone and brick and concrete
announcing whatever they announce to the world
and who knows perhaps long after this earth
    has gone silent and dry
and the rich houses by the bay have dissolved
    into dust and wind
lonely visitors will arrive from the outer galaxies
collect these forlorn pillars as treasures from the dirt
and take them back to fill museums in the void

the fragile promise of november
(for my father and his fellows: ww ii)

remembrance   icicle wind is a bayonets blade
jesus it howls   how many souls have been put to the sword
the veterans march with a muted pride
enacting their rite of death and recollection
broken men   old with saddened eyes
    faces scarred by this wild and drunken day
one wreath is blown from its stand
    toppling with an echo in the cenotaph silence
we are the dead someone says
we trim the empty tomb   to remind us where and when
in spite of all   the fighting goes on
    cruise missiles and cannonballs
here we coax memory   and fend the future
    like the mirror that reflects a mirror reflecting
the band stops playing
on the way home   straining against the blast
freezing against that fragile promise
    for my father and his fellows
defiant as tommy spit   there is a poppy in the mud

the poppy

the poppy fits november
    where the cold winds play

the red stands for blood
    and the sacrifice made

the black is for sorrow
    to remember and pray

once green was for hope
    but thats now gone away

o the poppy fits november
    where the cold winds play

day fine but sky cloudy
a tune for uncle willie, 219853

preface

i do not know how to start, willie, or where
you are so far gone and yet so close
    like a shooting star in its final descent
so little remains from your brief passage
    an old family photograph, a worn iron medal
    a letter to your sister, a slender stone
    an ocean away to mark your grave
and anyone who knew you is long past too
    memory of them now but a vapour trail
but from dusty attic boxes to the countrys archives
    in the found i find you   or is it you who finds me
raising your ghost arms up through that french dirt
and latching on as if the rhythm of the square
    had spun you into the arms
    of the prettiest girl from birds creek
and the rhyme of the holy fiddle
    matches the callers antic beat
and round and round you cling
as if your life depends on the dance
never letting go until the last fall of the music dies away
but i am here and wonder   what must i do
what slight part do i play in this grand waltz willie

i

perhaps that family photo from 1912 is the place to start
like so many photos of the time—formal, posed and stark
sudden prisoner locked in space by a local mages command
so stiff, and then
    like a howitzer lighting the sky over the somme
the sudden burst of potassium and magnesium
and you are stolen in reverse and brought to light again
preserved a hundred years for this tired eye, this old nephew
whose only war to fight was a cozy college contest or two
    a demand for better campus coffee
    or struggling to read the turn of the screw

in the photograph you stand rigid at the back
    encased in your sunday clothes
(we all know the feeling, willie—
wed rather be somewhere else in rolled-up sleeves)
but hair handsomely parted on the left
    and sweeping across your forehead
natty handkerchief jutting from your coat pocket
a five petalled badge like a forget-me-not
    on your stylish wide lapels
crisp-collared white shirt, charcoal black jacket and vest
a necktie pin that flashes in the flash
    —i bet you were the randy gossip
    of all the girls in town, willie—
your moustached father william to your left
    (at 15 you were obviously his right hand man)
your older sister mariah at your right
    her assuring hand on your shoulder
maternal janet, grim-faced in all her photos

      sits in front holding sarah in her lap
the other siblings—mary, mandy, mildred, george,
      emmaline, samuel, catherine—
(perhaps the numbers alone account for your stern
      look, janet)
all circled close with wide-eyed gaze straight ahead
as if hoping for the best but braced for the worst
with only brother clifford yet to come some four years later
a brother you would never meet
never fish the streams of lamable
or snicker over tales of the red-haired women
      come down from maynooth or in from
      the far reaches of dungannon and faraday
those red-haired women who came to town with a purpose
and swirled like earths paradise alive at the bancroft
      squares

ii

that photo, a dull pitted medal, and a letter to your sister
    mary, my grandmother
all thats left of a boy who never grew into a man
the letter written on yellow stationery supplied by the ymca
dated like that old joke in history
    it is from 'some where in france' nov 11 1916
two years before this masque would pause
    and rehearsal for the next begin

dear mary, you begin, I am well and hope you are the same
well dear I am writting this letter in the frunt trench
and their is some seris Bangs droping rather close
I will be glad when they move us back
    and I think that we are going to night
but I can say we have a fine officer in A company
and I seen a cupple Rats this morning
and I have a german button that I took of a stiff
    that was laying out in the Battlefield
and I have a pear of long Rubber boots
    and I am quite happy
well dear
I will write a long letter when I get Back to Billets
    so I will say good Bye from 219853
    Pte w a Smith 44 Batt BEF A coy. 3 platoon France
and there are thirty Xs in a tight circle
    —thirty paper kisses i suppose
thirty Xs to mark the spot, to affirm and affirm again
the hand, the heart and the breath
in a letter that arrived in bancroft
    two months after that breath was gone

iii

there has always been a battle of the somme
the ultimate river of subtraction by addition
from julius to henry to napolean and patton and on
soldiers move forward for a while and then are driven back
    the other side does the reverse
        a deadly dance of the ages
it was they say the first major offensive by britain
    in the great war (the greatest of oxymorons, surely)
and from july to november ten kilometres were gained
    along a 20 click stretch
and a million and a half soldiers lost
    sixty thousand british on the very first day
a swirling ballroom where the maxim guns played
    all day long and the 77s raved
even today, 100 years after, shells surface in those fields
    like spring stones in your garden
somme—the whole history of the world cannot contain
    a more ghastly word—wrote one german soldier

the war diaries do not say more than they have to
    but say enough
17-11-16 aircraft active   artillery normal
(*artillery normal*   what brings a human to such a
    statement i can only wonder)
sky clear and air cold   two OR killed   7 wounded
    and 1 missing reported to noon
during the night, snow fell
the tenth canadian infantry brigade carried out an operation
    this morning
the show was successful though mud in trenches

   retarded conditions
much exhausted casualties 1 officer killed
  1 OR killed 18 OR wounded and 1 missing
  several prisoners taken by brigade
and by afternoon the snow turned to rain
trenches in very bad state and men much exhausted
  have orders for relief
casualties in past 24 hours to midday today
  8 OR killed 7 wounded and 4 missing
day fine but sky cloudy

iv

the death certificate is carefully typed
    though not overly elaborate
i suppose with a million to type in five months
    the wonder is they had enough time, or paper

19-11-16. Died of wounds. No. 9 Gen. Hosp. Rouen
    (GSW. Head.)
buried in St. Seves Cemetery Extension
    Block 0 Plot 2 Row 8 Grave 7 (# 5545)

GSW. Head
o willie, you should have ducked
ducked the bullet, ducked the war
ducked the journey that took you so far away from home
you should have stayed in that fine black suit
    no matter how uncomfortable it was
it is sometimes hard not to wonder why we humans
    do the things we do
why i am doing this
why you decided from the remote hills of north hastings
    to join this soirèe far
instead of holding fire in the arms of those romping women
    in the squares of bancroft
what chords were played across your young soul
    to make you sashay to this bloody tango
the adventure of a lifes time perhaps
the pride of a pressed uniform
    and those spit and polished boots
    to charm the passers-by

revenge for the death of that old archduke
    (what the hells an archduke anyway)
to see the world perhaps
    the smoke and soot of southhampton
    the industrial clamour of le havre
    the french mud
    the bloody somme
my own father once told me he signed up for WW II
    because everyone else was
so maybe thats why you went
everyone else was going the whole world was going
the boys of bancroft off to stop the hun
    and bring the world to order once more

attested to this grand tarantella on oct 4 1915
chest   40 inches   complexion   dark
eyes   brown   hair   dark brown
distinctive marks   none
religious denomination   Presbyterian
fit to serve

V

o holy old bald head, willie, as all the locals used to say
    the girls that would have danced with you
what would you have become
    logger or banker or camp cook or miner
    lover and father and grandfather and patriarch
would you have been quiet and solitary
    or drunken loud and full of foolery

on that final day as the rain turned into snow
    and back again
i am sure you were as any of us would be
you would have cursed the weather
pulled on your long rubber boots
and then done what you had done each day before
    what you were told to do
others might get clipped but never you
    or your closest mates
        that was not for you
looking forward to the meagre plate of corned beef
    and turnip at charges end
and hoping the trench rumour was true
that you would be moving back for a couple days of relief
when you would write a longer letter to your dear sister
and then   sudden   from some direction
from out of barbed wire and trench and smoke
    and snow and rain
a seris Bang   a thud perhaps   GSW Head
and down to the mud
dark hair messed
    young light and all gone in those brown eyes
and human dreams vanished like the hopes of shooting stars

so far gone, willie, and yet so close
and i am left at best in wonder
have i done something of value
    in exhuming you in these words
have i done it well enough
no transcension to clouds of glory here
    no dull patriotic rant
no attempt to raise you above the rest
    or make your role more important
and yet all of those too   but mostly
you were a young lad from bancroft, canada
    who went to a faraway war and was killed
and conjuring what i can of your life denied
and how that was or might have been   seems important
and it is really all that i can do anyway
that and imagine joining you on a warm summers night
to drink a cup of spiked cider
    let the sounds of distant shells subside
and laugh together with the eager crowd just come to town
as the fiddler angel rises up and rests the rosin down

Notes:
Acronyms: BEF A coy—British Expeditionary
                      Force A Company
            OR—other rank
            GSW.Head—gunshot wound head

Quotation (re Somme): Friedrich Steinbrecher
                          (German Officer)

—William Anson Smith 1897–1916—

to see the queen

long ago on a warm falls day
me and my mom and my aunt irene
we got up early and headed out
we were going to see the queen

it was her first visit to canada
and i was so young and lean
but ive never forgot that merry day
when i went to see the queen

my uncle dropped the three of us
at the airports new gates pristine
and we stood and waited with the crowd
all come to see the queen

hours and hours stretched on and on
or so to a young toddler it seemed
as we stood and stood outside the gates
waiting to see the queen

then two mounties clipped to attention
and a black limo from the gates careened
and all the people cheered and waved
as the car shot past with the queen

we rode the bus back into town
and had a lunch of biscuit and beans
until my dad picked us up
and asked me had i seen the queen

of course i promptly answered him
as proud as ever ive been
just like everyone else this merry day
i had been to see the queen

now many times throughout my life
ive wondered what it means
moments like this that we never forget
when we venture to see the queen

and o the difference its made in me
im sure it has it seems
in how ive come to see the world
having been to see the queen

so please do not think too ill of me
if ever aloof or distant i seem
for once you know when i was young
i went to see the queen

alls right with the world
(Pierre-Auguste Renoir "By the Seashore" 1883)

renoirs lady wears a blue gown   silk and satin
    she wears a blue gown
and turns her head   lost nebula fixed   in grey cliff chaos
turns her head   her cerulean eyes   toward the painter
    her one true and only turpentine love
over her left shoulder and all around
    dark shades of sea slash in
shades   green yellow orange
    slash in over her left shoulder
and gulls disappear in the mist   their cries drowned
    by the spray thunder
boats balance indistinct   past a far white cliff
    on the indistinct horizon
in her right hand   long black needle at rest
tangled lap of pale yarn   formless of knit or purl
    formless as sea or sky before the bristle
and her other hand   clenched fist   a hint of anger
    of terror   a hint
the pursed red lips   the fixed sweet eyes
sweeter than any sky we could take in
    with mere human glance
search for something   something
    from her lover   her artist   her lover
    without him   would she not be   would we
something from her lover   who   i imagine
absolute artist   like all these absolute ones
    never lifts his eyes   from his work

cassandra ex vicis

bitch you call me   feminist
    and bury yourselves in the curls of your whore
blind men with white rods   eyes opaque as stolen marble
root through the night
     dream golden arms   and virgin smiles
walls unbroken   fruit heavy on the branch
think war in the gulf over
     agamemnon gone   bin laden dead
but fires that have burned are yet to burn
     old tired carpenters get new work orders
and another deeper ceremony invents itself
     new rituals   again
while you pray before steam and guts
     bow down to stone gods animated by old fire
you do not see the one in your midst
     seeing as you always never have
the price paid for scraping the sky   scorching the sand
bitch you call me   and leave me alone
     high in the rocks   the ashes of my altar cold
cursed in the fate of god and king
       prophecy is not an easy thing
       never quite yields winter to spring
naked   apollos smoky potion has done its work
for the rite i must deliver   i shiver   but i am
holy serpents have dug through me
     licked me clean   i see
dawn near its end   dew glistens on my pubic hair
     (no bikini wax here)   dew bristles on my thighs
i am teased without mercy by this new sun
     siring its singing sky

knowing more than any horny coker ever can
    liar of lyres
a time comes when like me   you   unbelieved   unadored
    a popcorn flicker in neon cape and tights
but there is no joy in this
    at least not as much as i had expected
silhouetted dark in the forsaken night   yellow bird sings
    from a thorny old tree
herald of greater death   and lesser
hail meryem meryem   blessed goddess and victim
    you will dream   a contrary dream
that will turn the sky violet with its bleeding
    and then youll turn over and dream anew
    sweet oil and that handsome nomad passing thru
but i am   not you
my premonitions miscarry me   always
what everyone wants to know that noone wants to know
a gods gift of love without feeling
    catastrophe *aneu* tragedy
i the psalm no-one sings
    a bag of bones   ash cold
you   disbelievers all   behind me   ahead   above
with bleary eyes   you tire from your evening revery
    and look to the future
        while silent ships come drifting in

beautiful sacrifice

i

the day she took sick   a pope died
for a year and a half
    the meds stopped the twitch of her left side
then that arm and leg went cold   distant
inside the cancer pushed on   westward ho
she always said it felt
    like the click of knitting needles in her head
and the neighbours stopped coming around or calling
in all it stretched out for nearly three years
another pope died and the shah and john wayne
and a one-legged kid hopped across the country
    and there was voyager
while this human who gave me life
    who worked and saved forever
    who had no knuckles in her thumbs
slowly decayed   like morning frost into winter
unable to remember the present   then forgetting the past
in the chronic care wing of the belleville general hospital
thinking herself back on the farm forty years ago
    or was it a million
amid the old men screaming   the old women wandering
    the stale reality of pureed food
and the rest of us waiting
    numbed by the caprice of a feckless guilt
like the condemned between the needle and the appeal

ii

during that time i remember going to see
    coppolas apocalypse now
        several times
where chef gets off the boat as it journeys up the river
goes searching for mangos
a tiger leaps from the jungle
    and chef barely escapes with his sanity
screaming his lesson   his conclusion into the night
never get off the boat   never leave the river

iii

the phone rang at noon
    i never thought that it would be at noon
        and summer too
and when i arrived at the hospital
her eyes were glazed and far away
that same expression i have seen in a cat or dog
    hit on the highway by some passing car
        the need to live no more
i held her left hand though it was paralysed and cold
and she died and the hand felt no different
    than when she had lived
and later the hearse like orpheus
    slid up and out of the cemetery
and the church women used her best china
    to serve a casual tea and store-bought cookies

iv

my father and i spread manure and grass seed on her grave
and now it is green   and needs regular cutting
and i sit far away   at a new job down 401
and smoke a pipe beneath the stars at night
where a breeze plays havoc with matches
    like the conscience of a tempest
and i try to remember my mother before the cancer
    but cannot
for it is a magical disease of the soul
a fit modern god who feasts on beautiful sacrifice
and transforms its saints into dragons
    and lovers into victims
who alone must fight to tame or to destroy
    merely to survive
to pray   to accept   gives birth to the demon
    the void creature
and in the first and darkest night of indulgence
we creep with knives to our own throats

V

    and so i wait   alone for a time
        quiet as the mangos that hang above
    to consider things and plan a path
        to observe and survey the landscape
    i think of molten lava flowing beneath the earths surface
        blood beneath the skin
    i think of people at the cinema laughing
    and i see the darkness   cat-like
        malingering   crawling forward
    sniffing the dead trail like traffic hunched on 401
    and suddenly   unsure   then sure
    i see myself stand   and step into the night
    and i hear myself screaming
    here   here i am   im here   im ready
    come and get me you fucking tiger

massacre at the metro: a ragtime tune

b b ribozzo
went to the metro
but didnt know what to do

so down at the metro
b b ribozzo
had a negro shine his shoe

slick angels zoot band
jived at the metro
a tune of debts and dues

and there at the metro
b b ribozzo
drank a starlights gin, or two

then b b ribozzo
danced at the metro
with the femme who seemed so blue

and the crowd there
doomed at the metro
became uneasy with his moves

but b b ribozzo
felt through the metro
a breeze burn strong and true

slick angels zoot band
broke at the metro
and in silence bade adieux

just as b b ribozzo
heard at the metro
big al say its time to groove

then down at the metro
b b ribozzo
let his light come shining through

    p.s. he killed them all, you know
        he killed them all

verge
(or... so you think youve had a bad day)

in the downpour   through the limestone city
    grey as grey is
i disembark   city bus slides away on a glassy path
    out to the mall
restless and wet between transfers
    i take casual refuge at agnes
    the campus art museum
where blind belisarius hangs on the wall
    the last of the romans
loyal commander to justinian
    passionate husband of antonina
now a great warrior with his wars all gone
    a general out of work
tried for corruption   eyes put out by emperors decree
cuckolded by his son   noones twisted twins
    left to wolves in the wood
imprisoned in byzantium   his armies taken over
    by narses the eunuch
belisarius does what he can   keeps on
    lives into his nineties
humbly holding his tin cup toward a passer-by
empty tin cup   blind passer-by

indecipherable students shout across lower campus
phones have gone silent in this deluge
a man in a yellow hard hat climbs a telephone pole
    slides down   climbs again
perhaps it is a sign   the verge of something
motionless i wait and watch from this dry place
    for the next bus in the storm

    i   already more educated than anyone needs
        yet still   neither this nor that
on my way to the bleakest of part-time summer jobs
thinking of a return to graduate school
        of forms to fill out
i brandish my transcript like a sword in the flood

by nine oclock   far away stars are clear   cold and still
but the candescent midway of the kingston fair
        conquers their sky
there is a music i do not hear   a scene unseen here
        where i bark a ring toss game none can win
crowds shuffle   couples arm in arm   young and old
        passers-by
watch the lights   play these games
        explore the mobile trailers anchored down
the gentle fair   the harnessed romp of the civil carnival
rhythms of a living apart   a distant   a yet to be perhaps
        or never

and then   silence
        pause for the split of a second
as high in the ferris wheel   plunging to earth
        a pregnant woman screams
blind belisarius is at the wheel
        and doing what i can   i fumble out this tin cup
            perhaps it is a sign

the passage of seasons

wes robinson died   up in the nursing home in bancroft
    my aunt ethel tells me
had you heard   he didnt know anyone at the end
    and only a few came to his funeral
your uncle jim was a pallbearer

morning   and breakfast   the mantel clock chimes
last lamable leaf has broken away   final autumn gesture
windows are expressionless   coated in steam
old wes robinsons cataract eyes
    all the clouds of a lifetime gathered
old wes was my grandparents handyman
forever a fixture in their cook-stove porch-mad house
    tottered on that hill in lamable   just south of bancroft
that world of sweet wood smoke rising
    and the wild fiddle of savage tait
    ever carousing with night in the valley
old wes   plaid shirts and suspenders
    logger and camp cook and tale-teller
    with gravel rochester-voice
knew more people and stories than i could imagine
    when i was a child
this morning   i can recall none of those
what i remember   he was always old to me   always
one of those souls who is old from the moment of birth i think
    and always full of laughter
old wes with red pocked face and ears burned off in the fire
    that took my grandfathers life
and years later   his tears interring his heart

      as he let my grandmothers coffin down
old wes who was always pipe smoke and rye
clothes and body and soul radiated these
as the eternal evenings of euchre stretched on
the more hands lost, the harder the cards hit the table
    and the stories never stopped

knuckles clenched
    that last laudable gravel breath escapes
      space by time broken   as always
old wes   didnt know anyone at the end im told
    freed finally of all the illusions
engulfed now in that earth season inconceivable
    beyond tale or card or fire or rye

the filaments are numbed lightning
    pale butter vanishes into the toast
the morning kettle trumpets
    instant coffee erases the cold throat like spring
each days wait brings mail in bancroft
    and the closing down of memory
my aunt and uncle are gone now too
    all that generation and their friends
there is no need to journey to lamable no more
the games of euchre over   fiddle silent is the valley night
the haunting chime of the mantel clock the final trump
faded linoleum moulded to the table and its empty chairs
a drift of snow
    hardened into summer blaze

heaven
(found poem)

the small child   the daughter of my separated friend
plays with a one-legged doll on the faded english carpet
and speaks of her life in tones free as air
she talks of god   as a bush with a beard
and of heaven as a forest   where christmas trees grow
when in church she says   praying faces are clouds
    in the stained glass sky
and we are all like arrows   about to be sent to heaven
where tucked-in   and street-wise
we arrive at the evergreen heart
a place where children cry no more
and legless dolls dance on rivers of light

barn fire

snow was brown as i were then
now   am distant fogged
pointing out to the insurance man
our hay elevator on loan to this unfortunate farmer

the barn after fiery copulation   deflated
sweaty spray did little to cool   the twisted bent elevator
even less for the yearlings trapped inside
smell was roast beef burnt
entrails of straw and chaff of oats left floating in
the distance
my back are turned with nights darting nuances
      to a single unity   to calm

morning   snow   again
      drifting in pregnant heaps over the land
recycled flesh   the boards and metal
      the blackened stone
awaiting a birth as before   but
no sun rises through the mourning clouds
no need for new barns in southern ontario

slowly in the bush   the farmer pisses   seen
      unwatched from the highway
the dead poplar leaves are orange   emulating fire
      rooted to the frozen earth
urine are warm   impotent   trying to put out the cold
even cold water melts ice

the deductible consumes any settlement   no surprise there
and i am now   today
and remember crumpled black barns and brokers
whenever i piss

eulogy for an exotic pet owner
(haiku)

he once said to me
there is nothing cuter
than a baby tiger

prehistoric literary note
(with apologies to wcw)

this is just
to let you know
i ate the plum
that was
in the refrigerator
which you
were probably saving
for lunch

forgive me
i wish i had
left it for you
it was as hard as
dinosaur shit

the storms of my parents

    i

crucifixes from my mothers childhood
    hung in the upstairs rooms
    with rosaries draped over them
and along the hallway she placed oval pictures of jesus
and portraits of our ancestors nobody knew

when it thundered   on those sweltering summer nights
my mother would wake us
have my brothers and i close each upstairs window
and unplug all the things we could
    electric clock   floor lamp   radio   tv
then we would sit in the kitchen
    coal oil lantern and a match ready
and wait for the storm to pass

she remembered her father long ago i suppose
    dying in a fire in a storm

ii

in the entrance hall my father hung
    tiny wooden shoes from holland
        and a silver belgian spoon
he also fixed there a german bayonet and cat-o-nine tails
'souvenirs' found on the grounds of a concentration camp
    near the black forest
where he said nazi insignia   eagle and swastika
drifted in piles along the barbed fences
    like windrows of mown straw across the earth
memento mori of the time of his youth i suppose

during the thunder   my father would pace the floor
shells bursting once again over monte casino
    cordite and smoke and the unspoken rest
each rip and rumble   each methodical footstep
echoing the war unended in his sky

iii

here in a highrise   many years later
my parents long dead
    all their sacred objects packed and stored
the lightning flashes and rain pounds
the thunder shakes my open apartment windows
and i sit   everything plugged in
    lights on   cell phone charging
    baseball game on television
and i remember when it thundered long ago
my brothers and i   waiting
    tired   restless   bored
together   the rain   the lightning   the thunder
the darkness
the storms of my parents   alive in my skull

asshole poem

once i read a book on tea
    and for half a year i was a tea expert
talking on and on to my friends
    about the subtle nuances of flavour
    among central and northern indian blends
talking jasmins   and darjeelings   and herbals
creating a tea philosophy   and a tea economics
    and a tea mathematics   until it was all tedious
and i became aware for the first time in my life perhaps
    that i was an asshole
a downright unmitigated pretentious boring self-deluded
    asshole
now this revelation was not all that pleasing
    but there was no denying it
and so i began to think about it
i realized that its a pretty important part of the body
without an asshole   (or two)   the world would be
    pretty constipated   plugged up
thered be no politicians to pass laws
    no lawyers to bend laws
    no criminals to break laws
thered be no bosses   no union leaders
    no principals or deans
    no cops (at least the ones who ticket me for speed)
no teachers like those you remember from your school days
no deconstructionist critics or those who read them
all the tv and radio talk shows would go silent
    and social media sites would fade away
and none would speak of rom or ram or terabyte
and so i came to realize that the world

    would be much different without assholes
and in fact as i look around year after year
    i feel less lonely in this place
and sometimes late at night   after a long day at work
after the evening news has offered its litany
    of perversity and destruction
i realize that everyone is an asshole   and i say so
    but quietly of course
so i wont cause any controversy   or upset anyone
    truth is a tough enema to swallow you know
and so i mind my own business
    offer up my simple nighttime prayer
    thanking god for her remarkable excretion
and continue my reading of a book ive just bought
by the way   if youve got a moment
have you ever noticed the elusive difference in bouquet
between colombian and brazilian lowland coffees

descent of species

over an afternoon session of beer
the biologist explains his theory
that one-celled life   amoebae and other protozoa
are really the highest beings on the evolutionary scale
never suffering from the weaknesses   of head and heart
up to 3 oclock   i vehemently disagree
    at 4 i offer a mild protest
        but by 5:30
            i am telling his theory back to him
and suddenly
    he is the one plagued with doubt

westview chapel on wonderland road
(for gary)

i

with emptied
pride
'thats my son'
he says
as in the coffin
we look
and like the words of some ancient book
he leans heavy on me

ii

in caskets
freshly dead humans
always look
smaller
fragile
like old porcelain
birds

iii

died in a dosage wreck
on his 21st birthday
some celebration
that turned out
to be

iv

he always wanted to be
a firefighter
now
fires burn
and there is no one here
to put them out

v

someone i dont know
thanks me for coming
and there is no air to breathe on wonderland road
god
this has turned into a difficult day

thunderbird bound in winter

    it is
windigo he hates
windigo against whom he spends decades planning revenge
windigo he fears just before he falls asleep

    it is
windigo who sends sister ice to cover beauty
an isinglass fog magic where cold bird shapes rise slowly
    and wing away
distorted as a mind chained to madness deep in the bay

windigo has many names
crow and coyote, auschwitz and tiananmen

windigo has many faces
all the hues of the deceiving rainbow, here, but not here
no beginning   no end

windigo often has a white face
and carries the thunderstick that kills
trades baubles that end worlds

    o sister ice
    break, crack and let me rise like a sudden cloud
    to set my peace upon the land
    trust me
    while IT sleeps
    we could change the world

while IT sleeps
i could embrace sky
again

free me sister ice
you need only break
yourself

it is
windigo he hates
windigo in every season
which now all seem the same

it is
windigo that he has forgotten
windigo
    that is his own name

Note:
In the old Cayuga stories, the name given to the modern
Bay of Quinte was "yo ya da do kenthe", which means beauty.

teenager

she makes love to me
      nonchalant as the fit of an old pair of bluejeans
afterward   i think of the old rituals told in tale
ancient rites fed by lust and blood and betrayal
the frightened heifer at the altar
      the penitent blade hovering

later i am startled awake   by a 3 oclock freight
she sleeps on   the alcohol of her breath like a shroud
and i hear the dark window rattling
old love-struck adam enchanted by first debutante you dine
blood shot rex mourning where clubby cock has been
even divine duncan jarred awake too early and too late
      the sleepless thane staring down

in the morning   coffee she has made is bitter
      and rain floods the streets
and when i drop her off near her parents home
she kisses me on the upper lip   thanks me for the drinks
      and leaves the car
i watch her go   motionless   rooted in neutral
delphinian teenager   fleeing in the downpour
her brief touch on my arm   jolt of an electric prod
antique prophecy   that howls the primal bone
and selfish as usual and afraid
i find tears in my eyes in the rain

guillotine troth
(from an a&e documentary on the brain)

for fifteen seconds　　　　after the oxygen goes
the brain lives on　　　　　so the surgeon shows

it sees and smells　　　　　and tastes and hears
remembers joys　　　　　　remembers fears

so after the blade　　　　　slashes thru
and the head is held up　　for all to view

i wonder what it knows　　what does it see
where would it rather　　　prefer to be

as it gazes over　　　　　　the crowd in mime
does it rage or cry　　　　　or lust a last time

some things i suppose　　we may never know
or only briefly　　　　　　　just before we go

but if it happens now　　　make one promise true
if you wave to me　　　　　i will wink at you

quarter days

another solstice   extreme geometry
    winters core at hand
it rains   hard veneer welds to yesterdays pristine snow
    like contacts on an embalmed eye
a sudden light in the chilly parlour   an elusive twinkle
and for an instant   one thinks the corpse alive
it is the artists season

my grade elevens finish their play in the christmas assembly
after a host of mindless skits
    after the keyless band has crucified silent night
their play was long   involved   with a message of sorts
and poorly received by the audience
forced to stay in school this last afternoon before holidays
the grade elevens   15   16   years of age
    on the edge of being older
show their emotions at the catcalls and shrieks
    disappointment   frustration   embarrassment   anger
they worked hard on this   practised long
    sure and proud of their gift
they have braved the public time of artists
    and found the season dark
it is a first small death   a simple sign of some thing to be
    like a forlorn birth in a shitty stall

i want to talk to them   shout to them from my own rage
    console them
tell them it is merely the way of things
it happened to me when i was them   and so many others
heart will come to such sights colder said the old priest
    lessons learned in rage and sorrow
    shape us harder for the morrow

this high school audience who cheers another skit
    where students pretend to puke at a christmas party
this audience on another quarter day
    will urge the whip that flays this holy babe
    will tend with care the gardenia orchards
        that decorate the burning places

and i want to tell the grade elevens
    in some way that they can understand
that the forces of creation must build beautiful things
    that must fall
and in dark storms gods with lipstick dalliant
    must hang on hooks
    or they are not gods at all
o my grade elevens   in your solstice
    in your triumph that feels like defeat
the sightless will swear they have no need of eyes
    rend yours from your face if you let them
it is your task to dance the brittle crust
risk burial in the hollow snow
summon a courage this wrestling mob may never know

most of all my grade elevens
i want to tell you   do not cease
the path you tread   guides them all
and one day
their dead eyes will blink awake in your angry palms

middle ages

in the shaft of moon   through the flower stained curtains
like some articulated movement   in the national ballet
the dark haired woman and i   make love
her dancing breasts deceiving the meagre light
    gyrations set to an ancient tune
and when it is finished   we rest beside each other
and caress each other
knowing, just knowing   that we have solved
in the vacant smile of the pale moons light
    the riddle of age and our dying

the hydro man
(from *The Prince of Leroy*)

Today, it is new. Eighteen floors of cement and steel and tinted glass. Pristine and shining in reflective sunlight. Proudly built by *Regent Construction*, subsidiary of Dalco Corp., and happily inhabited by the *Thornton Hydro Commission*, at last a place in which to consolidate all of its scattered offices. But in time, in fifty or maybe seventy-five years, it will no longer serve a purpose, it will be worn and used and need to be replaced. Perhaps they will do it by implosion. Where charges are placed and crowds gather at a safe distance and television cameras whir and the switch is thrown and puffs of smoke and dust roll out and, suicidal, the building abruptly sinks into itself like a concrete maelstrom. Perhaps by then, they will use some different method for demolition, perhaps some laser device that disintegrates cement and steel and tinted glass floor by floor so they can turn around and instantly build again. Perhaps, as some kind of publicity stunt, they will do a retro demolition. Truck in some great crane on loan from a museum with its huge metal ball stretching from a great steel cable smashing into the building again and again, blast after blast from the past.

Perhaps they will have to bring in trucks to carry away the concrete debris. And if they do, possibly as they near the end of the job, as they begin to truck away some of the cement and steel that composed the foundation of the building, perhaps one of the workers will notice something curious about one of the foundation blocks and take a closer look. There the worker may see, inside the broken concrete form, small open spaces and tubular channels, and inside these, old brittle sticks that, upon closer inspection, appear to be bones. The bones of a human body. A complete set of bones. Perhaps, like some homage to victims of ancient Pompeii, they will fill these spaces with plaster and flush out the form of a man from an earlier time. Possibly some poor worker trapped in the haste of erecting this old building. In all likelihood, some bored forensic anthropologist will be called upon to examine these bones, to flesh out their DNA and extrapolate a cause of death and a time of life. Perhaps he or she will find traces that indicate the onset of arthritis in the joints, and evidence of a left arm that was once fractured. No doubt, he or she will find the small hole in the back of the skull, perhaps even the small lead pellet still rattling around in the cranial cavity, which would suggest a violent death. Surmises will be made, and a cursory data check will ensue, and speculations will be uttered about famous people who went missing long ago—there will probably be Jimmy Hoffa jokes—and the case will be passed along to the homicide division and given a label and a number—the hydro man, unsolved case #313. A brief and intriguing curiosity. But then a pimp without a head will show up in an alley, and an eviscerated child in a yellow kimono will be pulled out of the river and the curious bones found in the old foundation will be set aside. A cold case. Filed away. No more time to be given.

There will be no record of the game winning home run he hit in Grade 8, of strawberry-haired and Irish Ramona Stewart, the first great love of his life, of the broken arm he suffered during that smash and grab at O'Neill's Jewellery Store (the glass in that case was a hell of a lot harder than it looked), of the six men he killed while working for Frederick Dalco, of the sad, sick feeling deep in the pit of his spine when Dalco Junior and his men cornered him in the municipal parking garage and he knew that they knew something they shouldn't, couldn't, of the brief second of disbelief beyond understanding when the muzzle touched the base of his skull. Of the hydro man, #313, beyond his DNA, and a probable cause of death, of Saint Paul Corrino as he had been named on the street, who many years ago double-crossed his boss, Frederick Dalco, and got caught, nothing more would be known. Cold cold case. Filed away in concrete and then in paper. No more time to be given.

universal concrete poem

C E   N T

C E M E N T

C E M E N T

C E   N T

S E M E N T

C E M E N T

C E   N T

a prayer for my students

i

as things wind down for me like some old fat clock
and time begins to tell me more than i tell time
schools and clubs, teams and faces rise
     like gaunt spirits from hungry yearbooks
teaching in five long decades, nearly forty years
forty years   and ten thousand students
ten thousand bodies full of energy and doubt
     and cockiness and wonder
and the conceit that they know it all, or nothing
     or dont care, or do
and they are always fifteen
year by year this talking body came to know
     the crease and ache of age
but they are always fifteen
     keeping us young and making us grow old
         at the same time, i suppose

ii

    after the banality of teachers college
        the artifice of imprinting on anothers classes
    and the passing rite of beer and beach, of ex and telethon
    sudden september is upon us
        yellow beasts with red eyes slip through morning fog
        prowling a young and disquiet jungle
    and i remember pausing on the sidewalk before the doors
        on that first morning
    'what have i gotten myself into'
        and then i push on, because i have to
    i remember my first class; most teachers do
    mine, a group of grade elevens emerging
        as all grade elevens do
    from childhoods placentic cartoon to the awe of a new and
        brave world
    a world of idea and insight and responsibility and freedom
        of body and mind
    where car keys rattle like rapture in the palm and tobacco
        is in the air
    where skipping a class is tempting as the illusion that free
        will affords
    where academic grind truly begins and a new light-just-met
        kindles—
        tom and tricia and dawn and terry-lynn and andrew and
        darlene and judy and debbie and ginny and mary and
        richard and bruce and dorothy and mark and barbara
        and chris and angela and paul and eric and nancy and
        rick and alan and kathy and rob and jill and tammy and
        dianne and catherine, and john (because theres always
        a john, and this one passed, though barely, because he
        despised the illogic of poetry and prospero but he liked
        the logic of grammar and that seemed enough at the
        time, and i have felt no regret since)

iii

a curious mixture of joy and sorrow sweeps over me
    one goes with the other in such matters, i guess
some flirted, some raged, some shared music and laughter
    and opinions about movies
some carried that dark chip on their soul
    as teenagers do best in building their moats and walls
some dropped by to say hi
    as i sat after school to mark or plan
some were probably wronged by me in some institutional
    way, but they managed to escape alive
some shared pizza at seasons end or coaxed
    this worlds worst dancer to their proms sway
some later brought their children to view the old relic
    who once taught them something years before
    —exactly what, well such is memorys blur
some slipped away when no monitor was in sight—
    one shot in a calgary bar
    one taken in an alcoholic car crash on highway 19
    one with cancer in the brain
    another whose double lung transplant didnt take
    yet another with sorrow on her wrists
        and nyquil in her belly
and some went on to deal darkness and consume shadows
    our world demands that too
        for the race that allows only one runner
            is no race at all
        success for every student is the pledge
        whatever that may be is the prize
most i believe found the benchmark
    that our culture demands of its systems

websites are filled with images of their families
     and friends and the revel of their lives
nurses and doctors and lawyers and police officers and
computer wizards and family makers and factory
workers and sales people and hollywood stars and so
many as teachers of course from my years at althouse
and all the rest

iv

and so in the end
what prayer do i have for these students passed
beyond the cliché of health and joy
what fear do i have if i have any fear
especially today when the world seems so stark
—bombs planted and towers dying
the rush of technology worshipped in every silicon of sand
and a carnival of misery
     aired as amusement across the land—
but of course time is no orphan, as all of us know—
drag that horse inside, nail the heretic to a tree
     smokes always rising where it shouldnt be—
the dark dogs of havoc have growled down the ages
     in different shapes, different dreams
like the ghost lines that faintly remained
     on all the blackboards i ever erased
     slight scars embracing each new day begun
so we take back the night and meet ourselves in the pitch
a prayer imprecise just whets the fangs of the bitch
     so think again   think again
what is the purpose of the bell rung, the hand raised
the poem, the equation, the experiment and lap run
field trip and science fair, debate fought and musical done
what the end in this hearts haunt of all these chalky rooms
but that these students received the power
     for their own prayer
placed true at their fingers touch
     whatever that touch can be
as near as minds echo or faiths will

V

and so my prayer then lies in its own souls way
after all the care you have been given
    after all the paths made bare
beyond the busy web find a pure space in the air
a space both genuine and fair
and be aware   with opened eye each day
    just be aware
and see it new   see you   and come to knowing
and the wonders of the gods will dance
like some magic firework that explodes again just as
    you think its done, and again
and you and your prayer will be one and true
    but always new
and so better the world too

that is my prayer
and then you must get on with the living of things
the swaddling of the babe
    the working of the sod
        the cheering of the wide tv
and this old teacher for one   illusion or no
will be satisfied to imagine his journey not entirely spent
or accord denied beyond the endless sere

pieces of a butterfly
(*for miriam*)

And there is but little difference in the manner of dying. To die is all. And death has been gallantly encountered by those who never beheld blood that was red, only its light azure seen through the veins. And to yield the ghost proudly and march out of your fortress with all the honours of war is not a thing of sinew and bone. Geoffry Hudson, the dwarf, died more bravely than Goliath, the giant; and the last end of a butterfly shames us all.
—Herman Melville *Mardi* V. 1, 9

i

it is not easy to grow old
    the old one smiled

        the white moth butterfly
        yellow egg   worm
        and cocoon brown fur
        awake—that ancient sorcery of the sun
        to live one day
        with powdery wings   and die
        one day as a butterfly

   so   you   crazy lady with your crazy laugh
my red haired elfin banshee
compatriot of a thousand storms and joys
gone now to live in tropic zones
where the jungly oceans sultry waves
    will sing for you
ride that surf
    let your sun burn hot
from dog to descent   love to loss
our time is made of such passings
we dance the waltz entropic

and here   at the end of my summer
where fiercest light dies
    in the falling thunders echo
darkness endures   horizon to horizon
but then   then
    a tiny quill of light pierces the clouds ink
and the sky cracks open again
    all not gone not all
and i retreat to the county and its deep mystic bay
where the breath of my ancestors
    still hangs in the air
where they rest loyal in this their dirt
    satisfied with the place they chose
satisfied with this green and fertile jut of earth
    with this place and this moody mystic bay

a fickle breeze teases puccinis melody from the
    rusting wind chime in the cob-webbed corner
        bringing the outside in
then silence again   then a tone   then

        last night   bed
        silver wings in my head
        morning   rise
        even thunderbirds have tumbled from the sky

who needs to believe in the book of faces needs
it was never i
though now realize
sight sees slower
and lone joints ache in the rise

    but

        still

        the horny dandelions
        overtaking the sidewalk
        can become armies   mad robots
        the acrid coffee
        a cawing jay   or   rusted knights
        quaffing at some broken motel counter
        drowning their thirst in quest of holy well

childlike laughter   from across the road
drunken sirens   beckoning   tempting
deep as sky   blue as sea
really nothing to worry about   they say to me
another beer by the bony pool   & rock n roll
youve done enough   enough   really
the day comes close   surely
when you will get no older   so   so what
no matter all of this   no matter   all
let go   i cant
you can   youve earned rest   maybe
sweet rest   may be one day
now sweet rest   now   no   no
          no
              still

          i know the butterfly
          riding currents of sexy air
          above the crawling brook
          dancing in the sudden moment
          pushing the stars away

it is not easy to grow old

praecipitandus est liber spiritus

not some monarch the painters fist
but no longer a caterpillar green
the white moth quivers   a stutter in the petal
    the flutter of light from the eye
fear   surmise   some hellish tour guide
    distraction by the smile of the adroit apprentice
    no   no rituals of death or polite applause
    no thank you notes for flowers
        laurel or biscuit and wine
sense and hope and terror like dust in the rain drops fall
    like frost on the blossom
the sacrament   then   a kiss (i think)
        the coy deception of twilight
feeling a warmth too distant
and knowing   just knowing
it is not the nothing   but the not nothing
the will   the sacred spell   remain like desire in the knot
lesser now but still poignant things
    greater perhaps in their very ebb
for when (after) all is said and done
    there will always be more to say and do
        but not me   not me to you
and even if one could
what use in seeing a world going after when

      powder is (already) caked
      and peeling like stale shingles
      from wingtips
where the darkest sleep erases the farthest dream
we become the magic sleight of what we are
that anagogic song and dance act who slips the fleshy ditch
    and wails   just wails   then
memory   mortality   the blackness   the word itself
gone in a whiff of dusk

the butterfly flaps silently
out of the night time
into the psyches shade
as much myth as human
trying

the prime sonnets

–canada and its prime ministers–

for my lab Melville
who lay at my feet in her dying days
snorting and farting and dreaming
while i wrote these sonnets
(and for Jazz, her sister, too)

prologue

*let us keep in our hearts the thought
canada first, canada forever, nothing but canada
—speech by sir wilfrid laurier 1900*

rugged hawk that carves adamant across the big sky
and scatters the primal jack along its chiselled lakes
arcanum of diamond and nickel and atomic gold
provider of loam, lumber and homestead, of port and grave
chondrite in timeless mime, unflinching as god on a
    breakaway

know well that first slight minuet, herald of wilder
    measures to be
blank tarantic blank slamming against flower, field, fire
    and flesh
twisting itself in progressive metaphor no poet could
    muster
nor seven weave exact; taken and taker, artifice and artist
    assimilate
a frozen shroud fluid as mourners at the ball

children at play wrap dark stones inside pressed snowballs
and cast them like coureurs errant across the stoic land
against the infinite finite of this absurd bush the still
    loon calls
as we seek some mental clearing and try to understand

the grand old cat

man must become myth, be myth-man
join one to the other to forge the land
—letter by sir john a. macdonald to george-étienne cartier
       1875

I could lick him quicker than hell could scorch a feather
—house of commons comment, sir john toward donald
       smith 1878

the limestone axis hews its path and stays the course
true as the northern star, firm as bone beneath the skin
such a compact teases a crazy tune, singular, seering,
       nuptial
as a spike; east and west with an iron handshake and a
       merry jest
toil and the right are the proper weal of the human soul

sometimes the winds of kingston blow against the sail
and even the great ships tack one way to get another
merciful heaven itself fears the human fate in an age
       of steam
cannons of destiny to the south, scandal in the park
       and chaos west
the miserable half-breed will swing though all the
       french dogs bark

a subject born to die a subject or never die at all
this, as much distance as place, succumbs to order
    and to keep
in a fifth of gin, some hidden coin and fire from
    rail and ball
and ever silenced bells on sussex ease an old
    unquiet sleep

one stone

however narrow and inexperienced he may be, I imagine he is a thoroughly upright, well-principled, and well-meaning man
—governor general dufferin on first meeting mackenzie 1873

logic sometimes has very little to do with political action
—house of commons speech by sandy mackenzie 1875

the truth, the truth must be told
I ha' no faith in pretensions any less bold
—house of commons speech by sandy mackenzie 1878

oh, tak' me home
—mackenzie's final whispered words april 1892

one stone, one stone, one stone, one stone, one stone, one
    stone
and sublime in the touch to let line be whorl—thats how
    the martellos were built
circles of stone ancient as time, guardians holy to the heart
    of this land
and thats how the buildings of souwesto went up
with gods grace in the face of it all to outlast a hundred
    generations

type on the page works the same way, one letter then the
    next
encode the law at its highest level and level the field for all
secret vote, redcoat riders, a college for war, free trade
    when its fair
principles that guide the hand free the body and save the
    soul
only then can we possess this land as it possesses us

caution kills the king they say who never dares to yield or
    roam
o mason of stone plying your craft, a slurry too strong is
    weak
finally stroke-swindled, betrayed shadow in their midst—o
    tak me home
but fore I go—fuck thee in scottish or whatever tongue ye
    speak

lights in the north

I hate politics and I shun fame
this is not my place not my game
—diary of sir john abbott 1891

why should I go where the doing of public work will only make me hated
where I can gain reputation and credit by practising arts which I detest...
—senate speech john abbot 1892

divinity resides in the palm of the father
not in the strum of a zealous guitar
the stories told in the words of the village
speak to the child of just who we are
settle in the heart and call out the stars

good men died so the plains could fall
and widows weep at the graves of sons
who cleared the land, heard the wild geese call
and made dominion over all in work and play
even god wears orange on the queens birthday

but the syrup tastes sweet from the green maple tree
spread on bread fresh made from old daves red wheat
see the lights in the north dance on without care
and the sun as it sets casts glory everywhere

o my annie

these yankee politicians are the lowest race of thieves in existence
—letter to annie from sir john thompson 1887

I wish I could be with you for one ten minutes to talk
   square to you
win or lose they cannot keep you from me much longer
you must not be such an awful baby until you get home
and then I'll see how far you can be indulged
—letter coded in pitman shorthand from annie to 'her
   kitten' john thompson 1882

though four little mounds scar the near hillside
whether the trees lean green or red
our five bairn shout in joy at eventide
and i see you walking through the golden barley
walking as you did when we were young

french or english, holy wine or transmuted blood
a land of plenty under one beating soul
or ragamuffin patches stitched by a steely thread
time heals wounds we hear even when children pass
may god grant us time for a wound a poor nation makes

if healing this land were true as our faith-crossed love
one slight glance from east to west through eyes so blue
would set the plaster forever; o my annie i pray
a luncheon with the queen then ill be home to you

printers devil

I sympathize, as much as any man can, with the minority ...
but I am not in favour of separate schools
—senate speech by sir mackenzie bowell 1895

if a man believes in one particular principle or one
    particular creed
and thinks it is the best
it is not for me to interfere with his conscience
—house of commons speech by sir mackenzie bowell 1896

bowell's sudden and unlooked-for elevation visibly turned
    his head
a ministry without unity or cohesion
became a spectacle to the world, to angels and to men
I never recall these days without a blush...
—joseph pope cabinet clerk memoir 1930

grand master of the continents sacred sign
plumed knight of her majestys enduring command
farewell my moira, you old river you, accepted and free
slipping through those wild rocky counties, ordering chaos
and sighing like a quiet cantation into mystic quinte bay

appointed when frog or dogan or pervert wouldnt do
here where the river is a rude and savage thing
hardly made civil by canal or lock or closure
this nest of traitors wants a split god solved
in the rumble of steel across a lone prairie night

nothing good ever comes from dumb belleville
where that beguiling old river of old sorrow weeps
while drunken trains chuff steady to far plain and hill
like the bays dark thunderbird bound, know deeper and
    deep

the ram of cumberland

the human mind naturally adapts itself
to the position it's inclined
the most gigantic intellect may be dwarfed
by being cabin'd, cribbed or confined
—house of commons speech by sir charles tupper 1890

she was by far the most attractive one at the gala
a bright blue dress and eyes of the same hue drew me
    across the room
I was quite amused to find after I had seated myself
and talked to her for some time about our favourite songs
    and singers and other trifles
that the elderly gentleman seated to her right was indeed
    her husband
—sir charles tupper life and letters 1916

i did ishbel on the dock while her husband sailed to port
and priscilla in the graveyard when the moon eclipsed
    the sun
dolly was a blessing in the alcove of the court
and sophia and her sister in the barn beneath the forge
and katherine anywhere a skirt could ride the floor

maritime medicos dont need to know very much
practice by snatching a body or two, thats what i do
and the affairs of man and state are really the same
make me an offer here and ill make a deal there
a joint merge will surely be found, if not by treaty
    then by sound

franny and ive been wed in bliss for over fifty years
outlasted by far all the rumours, the turmoil and the tears
so defeat by these bastards is but a small trial
besides i hear wilfs niece bears a sweet french smile

sunny ways

the demon of discord is in the land
blowing the wind of strife over all and in all directions
—speech by sir wilfrid laurier 1896

men are neither angels nor demons—
but beings endowed with some faults, and much more—
many qualities of heart and mind
—letter by sir wilfrid laurier to a friend 1898

pillar of fire by night, pillar of cloud by day
a jingo here on the farm, separatist there in the town
railroads to the future or armies to the past
no matter which path you follow
it will be strewn with pain and sorrow

the quiet of the library on warm weekday afternoons
the tolling of the matin bell from a steeple far above
between empire and eagle locked and cultures hardly one
the middle road we choose to take pleases almost none
but this everlasting no will make next century ours

the tie pin must be straight and true as le sapin
poise in silk chapeau and waistcoat of royal blue
to stride with an air both imperial and pure laine
let all know 'i am a canadian' merci beaucoup

equality of sacrifice

robbie borden took his acts
and gave our freedom 60,000 whacks
—old québécois nursery rhyme (trans.)

political partisanship is closely allied with absolute
stupidity
—memoirs sir robert borden 1935

the price of being a nation comes with a costly cost
dreadnoughts and taxes and eyes that wont dry
boys must grow into men no matter the language they speak
though the parting of the ways is nigh, we shall not break
our sacred pledge to god, empire, king or self

in flanders fields the soldiers lie broken
like young larks who fell too early from the nest
what war is this where these foreign men
hurl our precious souls to mud and that mustard sea
and at four shrug their tedium over biscuit and tea

the returned men are restless, the west is on strike
quebecs in a fury, our nations not right
but the world is at peace, we held our head high—
you must do what you must when cannonballs fly

old virtues

*when britain's message came
then canada should have said
ready aye ready we stand by you
—speech by arthur meighen 1922*

*thousands of people are mentally chasing rainbows
striving for the unattainable, anxious to better their lot
but unwilling to do it in the old-fashioned way by hard honest effort
—speech by arthur meighen 1919*

in winter the land is a noble thing
level and crisp as far as you see
stripped clear the trees they cannot hide
their plots of summer, anger and pride
enthralled in leafless comfort along the hillside

the swarmy pests of summer stain bush and rock red
and fire wobbly passions in word and deed
a nation of snow maddens in aestival heat
shingle-bob women dance in the summer street
and whispers fill the night with a smugglers gall

friends, westerners, quebecers, canadians
listen to me, the true geometric of sense ushers our way
a nations ends serve the means that it takes
only fools arent ready, aye ready, for such wisdom, i say

bonfire in the deluge

there is a good time coming ...
I come to call the sinners, not the righteous
I nail the flag of progress to the mast-head
I summon the power of the state to its support
—election campaign r. b. bennett 1930

if we cannot abolish the dole
we should abolish the system
—radio speech by r. b. bennett 1935

ten thousand years ago came the snow a mile thick
and crushed the stone and lake and tree below
nothing withstood; the world itself was shorn away
glory itself was torn away in this holy offering of
    crystal-ice
an old lesson taught for times of tyrant and foe

trained as a principal never to smile in public
and sealing secrets that dare not speak a name
the asses and masses need fervour and sweat
their brew and their barnyards, burroughs and buggies
are the wages they earned lest they forget

a will to give, quicker to tell and harder to please
lone dick and sis mildred dance a dance so stiff
their 'flag of progress' flutters on a dusty breeze
and the times grind them gone like glacial drift

willy of the valley

... conscription if necessary, but not necessarily conscription
—plebiscite william lyon mackenzie king 1941

I would not give a single cent
to any tory government
—house of commons comment by william lyon
    mackenzie king 1930

no need unless need is needed
and only we decide on that
war and welfare and rule of self
will forge this home and native land
and give all of us all our place to stand

strolls downtown may be wasted time
but spirits rise in unusual places
wiry pat and lovely mom are wise and tender
and a riddled heart needs such companions
which a world beyond ruins seems rare to render

how will the far future remember me
table rap and tea leaves right now seem unclear
radio rex, grand rebel, champion of supreme country
or lone child lost in a fearful tapestry

loncle

you never had it so good
—campaign slogan louis st laurent 1949

for the best years in your life
—campaign slogan louis st laurent 1953

because the members of smaller nations are human beings
      just as are other people
because the era when the supermen of europe could govern
      the whole world
is coming pretty close to an end
—house of commons speech louis st laurent 1956

    from nanna bijou to the whales of gaspé
    the sea is tamed to rise and fall
    from spears bitter winds to the totems afar
    refulgent tar binds one to all
    and the last link is forged to the national chain

    fierce as the eyes of the rocket, demons lurk in the dark
    and frankensteins pal igor makes a cold war hot
    crazy hazels loose; priests of god are jailed cross the
        metal worlds
    beware who you talk to, beware what you say
    the snow may be fallout, do we live our last day

    all the building and healing seem frail in this scourge
    do they not know the age of supermen is spent
    suez and the gas pipe make an untimely surge
    and a marcelled prairie fire does in this old gent

the chief

I will make mistakes but I hope it may be said of me:
he wasn't always right;
sometimes he was on the wrong side;
but he was never on the side of wrong
—convention acceptance speech john diefenbaker 1956

I see a new canada, a canada of the north
a new vision, a new hope, a new soul for canada
—vision john diefenbaker 1958

they had always opposed me
—many speeches john diefenbaker 1948-1979

victory is sweetest when it comes sight unseen
when morning dawns and the tomb is clean
trains and tv and one country we see
from pelees marshy rock to the blue arctic ice
augured as one in this covenant of rights

leadership is a lonely thing
pricks aspire to kick down the acting king
missiles on the inside and missiles on the out
heartless the foe; they will fumble the state
as the underwear man knocks at the gate

when paul first set foot in philippi
heavens proud angels held bow and arrow high
this prairie storm that roared out its thunder
left the mark that lightning imagines on sky

mirrors

*the people of canada are free
every province of canada is free
canadians do not need to be liberated
—tv address lester b pearson 1967*

*politics is not magic, black white or otherwise
nor is it an exact science
politics is an art
the search for compromise without betrayal
above all service — not to the self —
if it becomes self-service, it is degrading
—campaign speech by lester b. pearson 1962*

country of peace, country so kind
country of maple smile and maple mind
bargaining here and mending so
trusted and praised wherever we go
country of rock, country of snow o

the national drum sounded coast to coast
identity was the issue to refine the most
more than red headed orphan or sams cold moil
far greater than vain generals folly or gerdas fling
the country and mike became the same thing

that rag which took so many words to weave
seemed ours in the very moment it unfurled
it was ours and we were its and now our world
donned a disguise which even we could believe

the rose

the answer is no to those who advocate separation rather
       than sharing
to those who advocate isolation rather than fellowship
to those who advocate pride rather than love
—speech by pierre elliot trudeau 1980

there's a lot of bleeding hearts around
that just don't like to see people with helmets and guns
all I can say is go ahead and bleed
—interview pierre elliot trudeau 1970

the style is the man himself
—comment by pierre elliot trudeau 1972

the expo of love was still in the air
with pauls wild stab soon to be a mythic mark
but bad trips joined good in their beady ways
spectral cells manifestoed an end of days
this gypsy swinger of rude grace shrugged, and we watched

love conquers pride in this game of state
even if love needs hard measures to compensate
you cant eat just icing and have distinct cake
the long knives came out in a very dark night
the universe unfolded its inexorable flight

the queen signed off; the charter had teeth
the rose walked in the snow and paddled away
arose in extreme times, both beloved and pariah
when the nation demanded a hippie messiah

ahead of time

we will not take this nation by storm,
*   by stealth, or by surprise*
we will win it by work
—convention speech joe clark 1976

long enough to conceive,
just not long enough to deliver
—john crosbie on the nine-month duration of joe clark's
*   government 1980*

jerusalem is a very holy city
an embassy there makes good sense
indias totality seems marred with cowshit
and that powder blue suit seems a strange fit
man and luggage lost along a short trip

hard work and a coke gets the day done
distrust words that are too grandiose
substance not image is what people need
honest and common is the who they will heed
just trust the voters as the chief did before

nation of communities next to each
ahead of his time he claimed to be
but from petro plan to the death of meech
the time seemed never quite to agree

prepared

my time is now and now is no time for mellow men
—john turner, liberal convention 1968

because of my political views, I've been targeted as a
  lightning rod
someone who's too far out there
—john turner campaign 1984

I've told you and I've told the Canadian people,
  Mr. Mulroney, that I had no option
—debate john turner 1984

the commons of oxford are cool and serene
and oarsmen stroke steady beyond the green
prepare for a time, prepare for a while
and prepare once again that politic smile
until none is more perfect to bear the crown

sad donovan strummed in dylans day
a faint tune that but mimed the jesters howl
the finest honed athlete begins to fade
as seasons pass decade by decade
the only sound at the end, one hand slapping

beautiful, radical man of the time
but times they change as always they do
i had no option his resonant chime
defined a life lost, tangled up in blue

open for business

canada is open for business and trade
come on up, your free chance to raid
—speech to wall street by brian mulroney 1984

I'll tell you what my mother would do
she'd wash your mouth out with soap
—debate brian mulroney 1988

politics is always an intricate sport
whether contested across bench, bar or bed
we expect fates of nations to turn in a play
and we train politicians as jocks of deceit
but they should never appear that way

revolution was the call in these rainy acid days
and change needed in every device
super relations end neighbourly strife
sold by sacred trust and a perky wife
free trade, charlottetown and a 'roll of the dice'

time may change the thoughts we think
history truly has a fuddled way
but i wonder, were those irish eyes still smiling
as 'enemies of canada' stole your myth away

freak

the truth is that girls without mothers are freaks
—recollection by kim campbell 1992

charisma without substance is a dangerous thing
—speech by kim campbell 1993

who needs a leadership race
I'll just stage a military coup
don't mess with me I have tanks
—speech by minister of national defence kim campbell
    1993

the harvest moon hovers like beauty at rest
while ripe things are guillotined at will
dead leaves burn brightly on smoky hills
and with a blond smile a novice frost kills
such riven heart the awe in nature, in human ill

candid and frugal, distinct diamond among zircons
but divergent views really garner few thanks
difference is preached but conformity prayed
a legacy too gucci, brash to the ranks
soon a shell without shells, this woman of tanks

though the era desired new and improved
in can or box or bones
it still wanted its kittens coy and demure
not bred of ice and stones

smile of a tiger

the little guy from shawinigan
always seems ready to win again
—contemporary québécois nursery rhyme (trans.)

for me pepper I put it on my plate
—interview john chrétien 1997

technologys on steroids in byte and bit
my thought can be sent before i think it
the world a circus of prayer and bomb
temperature rising in mood and degrees
a thousand satellites and nothing sees

seize that thug by the throat and push him away
wave a red book in darkness to fend off prey
the strength of simplicity, raw soul of the street
a gristly passion sembled hard and so smart
breillon man weaves charms seeming straight from
    the heart

a 'oui' to depart nearly ignored from the manse
intervened on the brink, won by glacial chance
still all politicians might craft in his way
an earthbound true grit that swaggered the day

family dreams

if mr. harper wants to play sheriff, he can start
  by slipping handcuffs on himself
—*paul martin, election campaign 2004*

I rise today in support of the civil marriage act
I rise in support of a canada in which liberties are
  safeguarded, rights are protected
and all the people of the land are treated as equals
  under the law
—*paul martin, parliamentary debate 2005*

shadows are insubstantial things but still darken sun and
  spaniels
dagwood and dithers and a reign of kings overshadowed
  by sponsorship scandals
—*political cartoon caption on paul martin and*
  contemporaries new yorker 2005

private enterprise does what it does
and floats on its very own sea
charts its own course, balanced and shrewd
amid mergers and bribes and chicanery
casuistry calculated in each quarters return

our mad prophet would certain have smiled if he knew
métis blood finally conquering the land
success for a political family tried and true
but faithful gains among partners and marriage freed
were soon bankrupted by the business of human greed

be careful what it is that you wish for
that old adage has often been said
sometimes the dreams we most desire
lead but to realms of the living dead

our dictatorship benign

although we like to think of ourselves as living in a mature democracy, we live, instead, in something little better than a benign dictatorship ... for canadian democracy to mature, canadian citizens must face the facts ... and update our political structures to reflect the diverse political aspirations of our diverse communities.
—*"our benign dictatorship" by stephen harper, tom flanagan 1997*

I get high with a little help from my friends
—*stephen harper singing at the national arts' centre 2009*

from reach for the top to the fool on the hill
the one member of substance that rose from reform
though belinda walked and martin ran, theirs but
    a season ticket
on a one-way ride; a ubiquitous culture of defeat undone
and nation within nation at last made one

allemande right, sashay about, the west wants in, the west
    wants out
dosido the press, prorogue all doubt, your partners bow,
    then spin and tout, spin and tout
missionaries, christians, combat gunners too, international
    hellabaloo
tough on crime, and on the arts, tougher too if you happen
    to be poor
allemande right, promenade the night, the venerable senate
    is a house of whores

to appear at once wrong and right in those elusive quantal
    spots of time

slick slick sleight or via verus, only the deepest of magi
    might conjure that muse
like a simile pure, like an ancestral prophecy of some
    hallowed future tune
a joyous carol of freedom or a perfect dirge of the country
    blues

epilogue

what the country needs is not the fist of the pugilist
but the hand of the physician
the knowing and the balancing of rock and snow
—campaign speech by william lyon mackenzie king 1935

the nation sails on through storm and calm
too vast for a vision, too varied for rules
both a potlatch of the wise and a schooner of fools
always more than is heard, less than is said
the gist of its living and a sum of its dead

the leaders who led did what they could
sometimes by accident, sometimes by good
zealots and despots never closed in on power
cowboys and movie stars never got to the tower
the true north would not entertain such folly

the times themselves often held the sway
over what could be done and in what way
and through it all, this human clamour and blur
the rock held firm and the snow returned pure

Afterwords

—A Note on the Canadian Sonnet—

language is not only the vehicle of thought
it is part of the texture, inseparable from thought itself
—memoirs arthur meighen 1951

The Sonnet: The poetic form known as the sonnet comes with many traditions and conventions—schemes of rhyme and rhythm, a usual length of fourteen lines, compactness and cleverness of idea and phrase, content which is frequently topical, and a set of divisions in which one section of the sonnet raises an issue, poses a question or sets a scene, and another section ultimately provides a response. Although there are variations, the two most traditionally recognized forms of the sonnet are the Italian and the English. In the Italian sonnet (Petrarch is most associated with these), a problem or issue is typically raised in the first eight lines (the *octave*) and a solution or resolution is provided in the final six (the *sestet*). In the English sonnet (honed by Shakespeare), the first four lines or quartet generally presents the issue or problem, the next quartet restates or expounds on this issue, and a third quartet does the same. Then, because he is Shakespeare and he can, the grand solution or resolution is provided in a mere couplet (Shakespeare's couplets dazzle).

A Canadian Sonnet: The question occurred to me, if Italy and England can have their own distinct sonnet form, why not

Canada? Many Canadian poets have written many excellent sonnets, of course, most using the traditional formats, some inventing experimental forms, but none developing a particularly logical or consistent approach. The key questions remained for me—what might a true Canadian sonnet look like, and why? Surely a Canadian sonnet would reflect our country, our people, our collective experience, in some fit manner. In being Canadian and in working for years with young Canadians, certain tendencies of the Canadian personality seemed persistent—and I am certainly not the first or only person to observe such traits. And while there are always exceptions to any stereotypical generalization, and beyond the ineffable surface tendencies of Canadians to be polite and quiet and peace keepers by reputation (in spite of some recent actions around the globe), the disposition that struck me most is the inclination of Canadians to avoid strident views, to be deferential, to try to see various sides of an issue and often to try to accommodate those various sides in discussion, in effect, to sit on the fence (sometimes having to build that fence in the first place). As Canadians, we have perfected the deferential art of reasoned indecision. I will not pursue any great speculation as to the origin of this tendency (it probably has to do with our somewhat photo-negative view of our identity, *not* being British and *not* being American, and/or with the tolerant diversity of our culture in general which has been multi-dimensional, prismatic from the get-go (that old mosaic)). There have been some exceptions, of course, but those have typically been the result of solitary forces that diverged from the national inclination. I should add (perhaps a very Canadian thing to do) that, in general, I think this disposition is a good thing—for the most part, for most, most often, Canada is a decent place to live. From this image of the Canadian then, the nature of what might be our true sonnet strong and free emerged. Instead of two parts, the sonnet of Canada would have three: the first would present one view or issue or scene; the second would offer an opposing or differing point of view or consideration; and the third would sit the fence, sometimes offering no resolution, sometimes straddling or balancing the first two problems, and sometimes offering an alternative view entirely. This would be a sonnet of many voices, internal and external. I proceeded accordingly in my writing. As to schemes of rhyme or rhythm, in the spirit of our modern/postmodern world, I have left them irregular, varied, balanced by a tone that is sometimes flippant or coy or humorous, sometimes quite serious, often tinged in irony.

The Prime Topic: Having found a form, potential subject matter seemed as illimitable as the nation itself—the sonnets could be on anything from love to time to death to pine trees to hockey pucks to beavers to bacon or tim bits, or anything else; but I wanted some kind of focus in order, ideally, to develop a somewhat coherent sequence of sonnets, hopefully on a general topic that could endure more than one poem. (I was not sure, for example, how many sonnets the stalwart moose could support, as stalwart, or even as conflicted, as that moose might be as it stands beside the highways of Newfoundland at night trying to make a decision! And so, *The Moose Sonnets* I leave to some other writer!) It was roughly at this point, in clearing out an old attic space, that I came across three or four books on the lives and achievements of Canada's prime ministers, and the subject and format seemed perfectly wedded—a sequence of Canadian sonnets on the historic leaders of the country, *The Prime Sonnets*. So I read the books, did some further research, and the sonnets emerged. One caveat (and, again, I guess a deferentially Canadian one at that)—please understand that these sonnets are not meant to be historical sketches, or mini-biographies, or short dramatic monologues, or critical exposes; mostly, they are simply impressions, creative snapshots of the person and the time in which that person rose to become the first minister of the land.

The Prime Ministers of Canada

Sir John A. Macdonald	1867-1873; 1876-1891
Alexander Mackenzie	1873-1878
Sir John Abbott	1891-1892
Sir John Thompson	1892-1894
Sir Mackenzie Bowell	1894-1896
Sir Charles Tupper	1896
Sir Wilfrid Laurier	1896-1911
Sir Robert Borden	1911-1920
Arthur Meighen	1920-1921; 1926
Richard B. Bennett	1930-1935
William Lyon Mackenzie King	1921-1926; 1926-1930; 1935-1948
Louis St. Laurent	1948-1857
John G. Diefenbaker	1957-1963
Lester B. Pearson	1963-1968
Pierre E. Trudeau	1968-1979; 1980-1984
Joe Clark	1979-1980
John Turner	1984
Brian Mulroney	1984-1993
Kim Campbell	1993
Jean Chrétien	1993-2003
Paul Martin	2003-2006
Stephen Harper	2006-

Author Bio Note:

Brian Thomas Wesley Way (*middle names, after his grandfathers*) was born and raised on a small farm in the north end of Prince Edward County, just south of Belleville, Ontario, a place where Loyalist ancestors came to settle in the1790s (John B. Way, grandfather three times great, actually built the original grist mill in the village of Ameliasburgh (then called Way's Mills), a mill long since dismantled and relocated to Black Creek Pioneer village in Toronto). Way attended S. S. # 6 Ameliasburgh Public School in the County (it, too, has been moved, at least in name, to Rednersville). He attended Belleville Collegiate (it was not moved—just demolished) and Queen's and Western, each of which remains in place, at least at this writing.

He has been involved throughout his life in education of various kinds, in secondary schools in Belleville, Tilsonburg, Ingersoll and London, in university at Western, and in college at Loyalist. Way has had scholarly articles and monographs published on a range of topics in education and literature—among those still of relevance, *Passages to Literature*, a series of teaching manuals, *Print Preview,* an undergraduate research and writing guide, and *The Fiction of Fishing*, a full-length critical study of the American metafictionist, Richard Brautigan, under review (a chapter was published in the recent issue of *Change* magazine).

Way recently returned to the north shore of Prince Edward County living in a small house on the poor (*aka* south) side of the road which he calls *Here*. He has served on the Board of Trustees for the *Prince Edward County Library and Archives*, as a member of the *Friends of the A-Frame*, a group involved in the preservation of Al Purdy's famed residence, and has recently been appointed to membership on the Board of Governors of the *Royal Military Colleges of Canada*. Currently, Way is in the process of translating his literary novel, *The Prince of Leroy*, into a screenplay  and an adventure tale, and *Orchard of the Gods*, a play about rural settlement, cultural displacement and mythic unrest, is under consideration by *Persephone Theatre*. Throughout his life, he has written and published poetry in a variety of magazines including *blackfish*, *The Canadian Forum*, *escorial*, *quarry*, *the pom seed*, *preserved thoughts*, *tamarack*, *sweven*, *waves*, *white pelican*. A memoir entitled *Hickory Tunes* and a collection of short fiction are also in the works.

As to the more personal and provocative aspects of Way's life, his wild romances, exotic global escapades and spiritual conversions, the details are intriguing, breathtaking, in fact, full of wonder...You know... as I write this, it is a dreary winter's day, heavy rain and thick fog rolling over the bay and settling against my Sunday morning window. And as usual, this outside weather is bringing on an inner change of climate, coaxing me to other, perhaps deeper, surely more useful pursuits than this solipsistic, self-serving bio. And besides, it's lunch time and there's a game on.

Enough.

Books in the North Shore Series
Find full information at
– http://www.HiddenBrookPress.com/b-NShore.html

2 Anthologies

Changing Ways is a book of prose by Cobourg area authors including: Jean Edgar Benitz, Patricia Calder, Fran O'Hara Campbell, Leonard D'Agostino, Shane Joseph, Brian Mullally. Editor: Jacob Hogeterp
  – Prose – ISBN – 978-1-897475-22-5

That Not Forgotten - Editor – Bruce Kauffman with 118 authors from the North Shore geographic area.
  – Prose and Poetry – ISBN – 978-1-897475-89-8

First set of five books

— M.E. Csamer – Kingston – *A Month Without Snow*
  – Prose – ISBN – 978-1-897475-87-2
— Elizabeth Greene – Kingston – *The Iron Shoes*
  – Poetry – ISBN – 978-1-897475-76-6
— Richard Grove – Brighton – *A Family Reunion*
  – Prose – ISBN – 978-1-897475-90-2
— R.D. Roy – Trenton – *A Pre emptive Kindness*
  – Prose – ISBN – 978-1-897475-80-3
— Eric Winter – Cobourg – *The Man In The Hat*
  – Poetry – ISBN – 978-1-897475-77-3

Second set of five books

— Janet Richards – Belleville – *Glass Skin*
  – Poetry – ISBN – 978-1-897475-01-0
— R.D. Roy – Trenton – *Three Cities*
  – Poetry – ISBN – 978-1-897475-96-4
— Wayne Schlepp – Cobourg – *The Darker Edges of the Sky*
  – Poetry – ISBN – 978-1-897475-99-5
— Benjamin Sheedy – Kingston – *A Centre in Which They Breed*
  – Poetry – ISBN – 978-1-897475-98-8
— Patricia Stone – Peterborough – *All Things Considered*
  – Prose – ISBN – 978-1-897475-04-1

Third set of five books

— Mark Clement – Cobourg – *Island In the Shadow*
  – Poetry – ISBN – 978-1-897475-08-9
— Anthony Donnelly – Brighton – *Fishbowl Fridays*
  – Prose – ISBN – 978-1-897475-02-7
— Chris Faiers – Marmora – *ZenRiver Poems & Haibun*
  – Poetry – ISBN – 978-1-897475-25-6
— Shane Joseph – Cobourg – *Fringe Dwellers* Second Edition
  – Prose – ISBN – 978-1-897475-44-7
— Deborah Panko – Cobourg – *Somewhat Elsewhere*
  – Poetry – ISBN – 978-1-897475-13-3

Forth set of five books

— Diane Dawber – Bath – *Driving, Braking and Getting out to Walk*
  – Poetry – ISBN – 978-1-897475-40-9
— Patrick Gray – Port Hope – *This Grace of Light*
  – Poetry – ISBN – 978-1-897475-34-8
— John Pigeau – Kingston – *The Nothing Waltz*
  – Prose – ISBN – 978-1-897475-37-9
— Mike Johnston – Cobourg – *Reflections Around the Sun*
  – Poetry – ISBN – 978-1-897475-38-6
— Kathryn MacDonald – Shannonville – *Calla & Édourd*
  – Prose – ISBN – 978-1-897475-39-3

Fifth set of three books

— Tara Kainer – Kingston – *When I Think On Your Lives*
  – Poetry– ISBN – 978-1-897475-68-3
— Morgan Wade – Kingston – *The Last Stoic*
  – Novel – ISBN – 978-1-897475-63-8
— Kathryn MacDonald – Shannonville – *A Breeze You Whisper*
  – Poetry – ISBN – 978-1-897475-66-9

Sixth set of three books

— Bruce Kauffman – Kingston – *The Texture of Days, in Ash and Leaf*
   – Poetry – ISBN – 978-1-897475-86-7
— Chris Faiers – Marmora – *Eel Pie Island Dharma: A hippie memoir/haibun*
   – A memoir in haibun form – ISBN - 978-1-897475-92-8
— Theodore Michael Christou – Kingston – *an overbearing eye*
   – Poetry – ISBN – 978-1-897475-93-5

Seventh set of four books

— Alyssa Cooper – Kingston – *Cold Breath of Life*
   – Poetry – ISBN – 978-1-927725-02-3
— Bruce Kauffman – Kingston – *The Silence Before the Whisper Comes*
   – Poetry – ISBN – 978-1-897475-98-0
— S.E. Richardson – Kingston – *Before I Lose Light*
   – Poetry – ISBN – 978-1-927725-05-4
— G. W. Rasberry – Kingston – *More Naked Than Ever*
   – Poetry – ISBN – 978-1-927725-04-7

Eighth set of six books

— Brian Way – Carrying Place – *redirection*
   – Poetry – ISBN – 978-1-927725-20-7
— David Pratt – Kingston – *Apprehensions of Van Gogh*
   – Poetry – ISBN – 978-1-927725-21-4
— Felicity Sidnell Reid – Colborne – *Alone*
   – Young Adult Novel – ISBN - 978-1-927725-18-4
— James Ronson – Port Hope – *Power and Possessions*
   – Novel – ISBN – 978-1-927725-22-1
— Morgan Wade – Kingston – *Bottle and Glass*
   – Novel – ISBN – 978-1-9227-19-1
— Jim Christy – Belleville – *Bad Day for Ralphie*
   – Short Stories – ISBN – 978-1-927725-23-8

www.ingramcontent.com/pod-product-compliance
Lightning Source LLC
Chambersburg PA
CBHW071523080526
44588CB00011B/1545